HUNTING: PURSUING WILD GAME!™

FALCONRY AND GAME HAWKING

Corona Brezina

rosen publishing's rosen central®
New York

Published in 2013 by The Rosen Publishing Group, Inc.
29 East 21st Street, New York, NY 10010

First Edition

Library of Congress Cataloging-in-Publication Data

Brezina, Corona.
Falconry and game hawking/Corona Brezina.
p. cm.—(Hunting—pursuing wild game)
Includes bibliographical references and index.
ISBN 978-1-4488-8279-3 (library binding)—
ISBN 978-1-4488-8285-4 (pbk.)—
ISBN 978-1-4488-8286-1 (6-pack)
1. Falconry—Juvenile literature. I. Title.
SK321.B69 2013
799.2'32—dc23

2012018511

Manufactured in the United States of America

CPSIA Compliance Information: Batch #W13YA: For further information, contact Rosen Publishing, New York, New York, at 1-800-237-9932.

On the cover: A falconer holds a peregrine falcon. Once an endangered species in the United States, peregrine falcons are now thriving and are known for their steep, swift dive when catching prey.

CONTENTS

INTRODUCTION

Picture a pond at the edge of a meadow at dawn, a flock of ducks bobbing on the surface. High above, unnoticed by the waterfowl, a peregrine falcon slowly circles. Suddenly, a human appears on the scene, running up and crashing through the reeds. The flock takes wing and then the falcon plunges, plummeting head first at a speed unmatched by any land animal, her wings folded back. The falcon hits one of the ducks in midair and the bird tumbles to the ground. The falcon settles down on the ground to tear into the prey with her beak and sharp talons. Shortly afterward, the falcon's handler catches up and swaps the duck for a piece of raw meat. Falcon on glove, he heads home. For the falconer and his bird, it has been a successful hunt.

Falconry is the practice of hunting wild game by means of a trained bird of prey. Falconry is both a sport and an art. It requires commitment, patience, and hard work. In practical terms, a falconer must be avid about the outdoors, enthusiastic about hunting, tenacious when frustrated by the bird's behavior, and open to learning new knowledge and skills. Many falconers claim that falconry is the most highly regulated of any sport. A prospective apprentice will fill out considerable paperwork before even acquiring a hawk.

Falcons are not pets. They are fierce, fearless, and determined predators that are supremely well adapted

A falconer extends his glove to provide his red-tailed hawk a landing perch. Raptors flown in falconry are trained to return to their handler.

to pursue and take down game. Moreover, they do not exhibit affection for their owners. The falconer and the falcon develop a close relationship, but it is a working relationship based on mutual trust and cooperation. A falconer learns to respect the falcon's abilities as a hunter. The falcon responds to the handler's cues and follows her natural instincts on the field. Together, the falconer and falcon cooperate during the hunt to take down wild game.

Experienced falconers often tell prospective apprentices that falconry can become more of a lifestyle than a pastime. They arrange their schedules around falconry and make sacrifices for the sport. Young people considering taking up falconry, however, must weigh whether they can balance such a demanding activity with school, extracurricular activities, and social life. For apprentices who do take up falconry, it can lead to a rewarding experience and a unique working partnership.

CHAPTER 1

AN ANCIENT ART

Archaeological evidence indicates that the practice of falconry dates back to at least the eighth century BCE in the Middle East. Some historians maintain that falconry began even earlier, as long ago as four thousand years ago, in Asia. Ancient peoples in China, Japan, Mongolia, Persia, and Egypt, as well as the Middle East, hunted game with hawks. Falconry reached Italy in the sixth century CE and was popular in England by the seventh century CE, when King Ethelbert II of Kent was an avid falconer.

During the Crusades, which began in the eleventh century, returning European fighters brought back exotic goods and advances in science and culture. In this way, new falconry practices reached Europe. Arabic falconers were—and still are—among the world's masters in the practice. Falconry remained hugely popular in Europe throughout the Middle Ages.

A page from an illuminated manuscript dating from 1304 depicts Conrad, Duke of Swabia (part of present-day Germany), hunting with a falcon.

Modern-day falconers take pride in falconry's long traditions. One of the most revered historical figures in falconry is Frederick II of Hohenstaufen, the Holy Roman emperor who reigned during the thirteenth century. Frederick II was a great supporter of arts and sciences who surrounded himself with scholars from across his realm and beyond, including expert falconers he brought back to Europe during a Crusade. Falconry was Frederick's greatest passion, and he is said to have once lost a battle when he left a siege site to go hawking. He spent forty years writing *De arte venandi cum avibus*, a six-volume treatise on falconry that described the hunting practices and biology of raptors.

An Aristocratic Pastime

Falconry during the Middle Ages served as a means of acquiring game, but more significantly, it provided a source of entertainment and sport. People from all classes pursued falconry—Shakespeare makes numerous references to falconry in his plays—and falcons served as status symbols among the nobility. Kings took their falconers and falcons along when they waged war. Prize falcons were included in treaty provisions. Falcons in England were strictly protected, with harsh penalties for poaching or stealing.

Members of royalty and high nobility generally employed falconers to train and handle their birds. The gyrfalcon, a large and powerful bird, was reputed to be particularly difficult to train. White gyrfalcons, which were especially prized, were captured in Greenland and transported to Europe.

A person's bird reflected his or her social status in medieval Europe. Ownership of birds was restricted according to one's position in the social order. The *Boke* [Book] *of Saint Albans*, written in 1486, contains a tract on falconry that lists the type of bird for each rank in society. The eagle was for the emperor. The gyrfalcon was for the king. Princes, earls, and barons flew different types of peregrine falcons. Knights flew the saker falcon, a large Eurasian bird, and squires flew a less highly regarded falcon called the lanner. "Milady's falcon"—the falcon for noblewomen—was the relatively small merlin. Lower social ranks flew other small raptors such as the goshawk, the hobby, the sparrow hawk, and the kestrel.

The royal hunt was an elaborate affair where members of the nobility and the falcons were tended by numerous servants who flushed the prey, transported the falcons, and retrieved the game. The larger falcons were flown after quarry such as herons, quail, and rooks. Merlins pursued skylarks.

Chinese hunters pose with their gyrfalcons, the world's biggest falcons, which inhabit far northern regions and prey on large birds such as ptarmigans.

Falconry's era waned in the late eighteenth century with social changes and the introduction of firearms. Although some falconers continued to preserve the tradition, falcons and falconry were no longer held in high prestige. Gamekeepers began viewing peregrine falcons as pests and attempted to eradicate them.

Falconry in the United States

Falconry did not take root in the United States until the twentieth century, when *National Geographic* published a few articles on falconry in the 1920s and 1930s. A few local falconry clubs were organized, and the North American Falconers Association (NAFA) was formed in 1961. During the 1970s, the group worked with the U.S. Fish and Wildlife Service to draft and enact federal standards governing falconry. These new rules legalized the sport and established strict regulations that protected both captive birds and wild populations.

During the 1960s, however, many falconers had begun to notice a decline in numbers of peregrine falcons. The cause was found to be a pesticide called DDT that caused a thinning of the birds' eggshells. The pesticide was banned, but peregrine populations had nearly vanished in the United States. Falconers were unwilling to allow the bird to go extinct. In 1968, a falconer named Larry Schramm raised the first peregrine chick in captivity in the United States. In 1972, biologist Tom Cade established the Peregrine Fund to support captive breeding efforts and hack back—or reintroduce—peregrines into the wild. Strongly supported by the falconry community, the recovery effort was such a success that the peregrine is no longer listed as endangered.

In the early 1980s, a scandal tarnished the image of falconry. The government set up a controversial undercover operation called Operation Falcon intended to catch falconers selling birds illegally on

A volunteer helps a biologist with the Peregrine Fund release Aplomado falcon fledglings onto ranch land in western Texas. They are using a hack tower especially designed for Aplomado falcons.

the international market. Sixty-eight people were convicted for breaking the law, but most were falconers who wanted to acquire a bird for personal use. Many falconers contended that the undercover agent entrapped would-be buyers by tempting them with repeated offers.

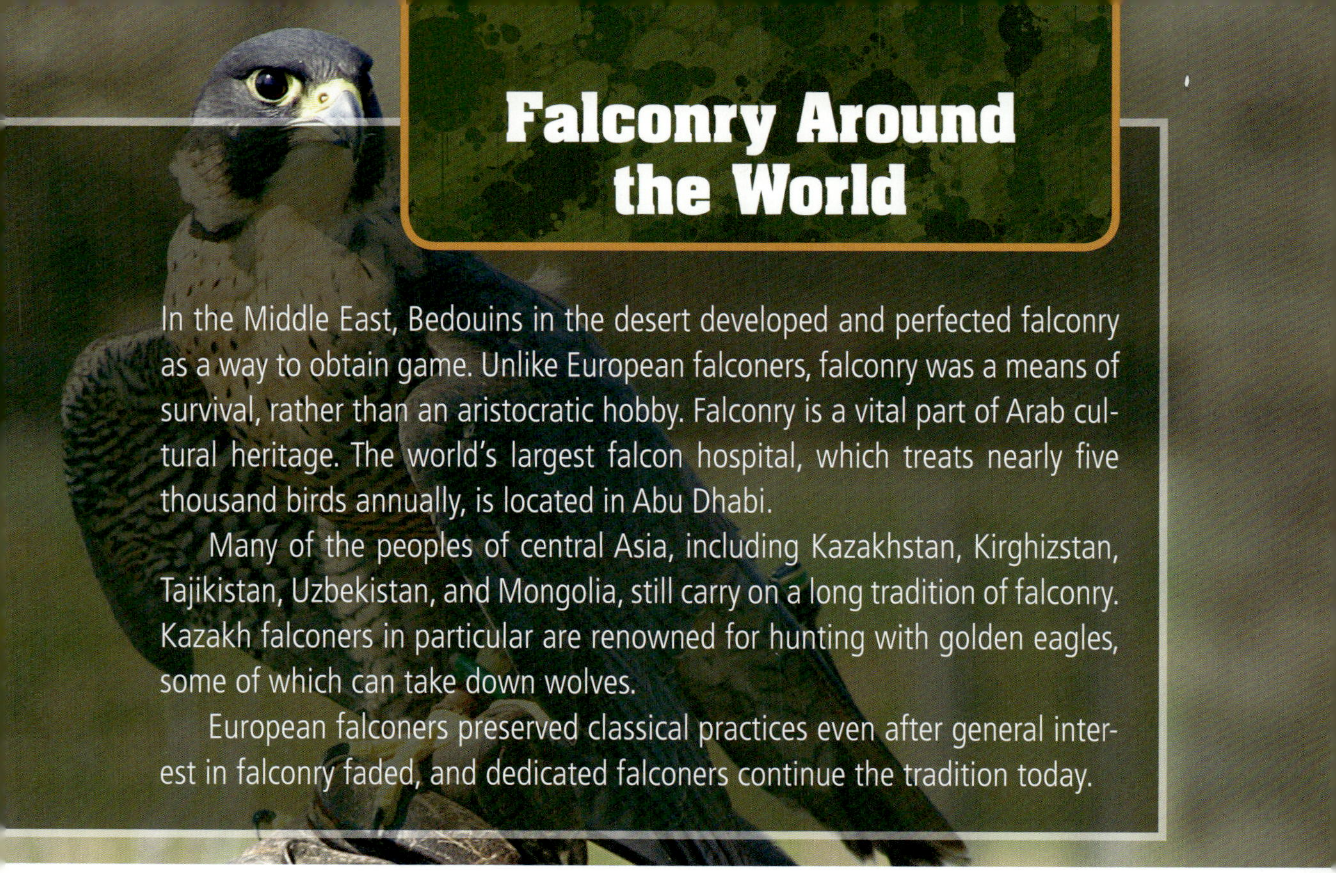

Falconry Around the World

In the Middle East, Bedouins in the desert developed and perfected falconry as a way to obtain game. Unlike European falconers, falconry was a means of survival, rather than an aristocratic hobby. Falconry is a vital part of Arab cultural heritage. The world's largest falcon hospital, which treats nearly five thousand birds annually, is located in Abu Dhabi.

Many of the peoples of central Asia, including Kazakhstan, Kirghizstan, Tajikistan, Uzbekistan, and Mongolia, still carry on a long tradition of falconry. Kazakh falconers in particular are renowned for hunting with golden eagles, some of which can take down wolves.

European falconers preserved classical practices even after general interest in falconry faded, and dedicated falconers continue the tradition today.

Old Traditions and Modern-Day Falconry

Today, there are about 4,500 falconers in the United States. Falconry still maintains significant legacies—beginning falconers are "apprentices," for example, and the highest level is "master falconer." Modern technology has allowed advances such as the breeding of hybrid birds and the development of improved tracking methods, but many everyday practices of taming, training, and flying falcons are still rooted in centuries-old methods. Much specialized falconry terminology dates back to medieval times.

One significant change has been in the expansion of captive breeding of falcons. Falconers no longer have to trap birds in the wild for use as hunting falcons, although many believe that those caught in the wild make superior hunting birds.

CHAPTER 2

GETTING TO KNOW YOUR FALCON

Raptors are carnivorous birds that, with the exception of vultures, pursue and kill their prey. Raptors, or birds of prey, include falcons, hawks, eagles, vultures, and owls. They range in size from huge condors (a type of vulture) that weigh more than 20 pounds (9 kilograms) to tiny sparrow-sized falconets. Female raptors are larger than males. The size difference is considerable in some species—a female sharp-shinned hawk can weigh nearly twice as much as a male.

All raptors have large, powerful talons and sharp, hooked beaks that they use to tear at meat. They have enormous eyes relative to their size, and a raptor's vision is about three times as keen as human sight. Raptors are known as fast fliers, with many species capable of diving at speeds of more than 100 miles per hour (150 kilometers per hour), but they are also extremely versatile fliers. In addition

A handler holds an Aplomado falcon, a medium-sized bird found primarily in South America that pursues small game birds. Thanks to the efforts of the Peregrine Fund, these falcons are being reintroduced in the southern region of the United States.

to plunging down for prey—or "stooping," in falconry terminology—they can soar, glide, hover, and engage in active flapping flight typical of all birds.

Not all raptors are flown in falconry. Vultures, for example, are scavengers and do not pursue prey. Owls can be trained for hunting, but because they are nocturnal, hunting with an owl is not practical.

Falconers categorize raptors used for hunting into "long wing" and "short wing" birds. Long-wing birds are the true falcons historically associated with the sport of falconry. Other groups of raptors used by falconers include buteos (such as the red-tailed hawk) and accipiters (such as the goshawk and Cooper's hawk). Falcons pursue game birds almost exclusively. The other types of raptors are generalized hunters, chasing prey such as rabbits and squirrels, as well as birds. There are slight differences in training and hunting techniques for different groups of birds, although practices are largely similar.

In strict falconry terminology, a "falcon" is a female peregrine falcon. A male falcon is a tiercel. Today, the term "falconry" generally describes game hunting with any type of raptor. It is used interchangeably with "hawking." A person who hunts exclusively with eagles or hawks is called an "austringer," although that term is no longer commonly used.

Peregrine Falcon

For many falconers, the peregrine falcon has no equal as a hunting bird. The peregrine weighs about 2 pounds (0.9 kg) and is about the size of a crow. Subspecies of the peregrine exist on all continents other than Antarctica, and it may be the world's most widespread bird of prey. Because of the effects of DDT, the eastern subspecies native to the United States has gone extinct. Three other subspecies are found across the country.

Falconers hunt game birds such as ducks and grouse with the peregrine. During the hunt, the peregrine tends to "wait on," or circle high overhead waiting for the falconer to flush quarry. Once in pursuit, she is capable of stunning aerial acrobatic maneuvers that are effective in countering evasive moves by the target. In the wild, peregrines sometimes hunt in pairs. During the hunt, the falconer stands in as the partner that flushes quarry for the peregrine to chase.

Red-tailed Hawk

The red-tailed hawk is one of the two raptors that apprentice falconers are widely permitted to fly. It is a large bird—the female can weigh more than 3 pounds (1.4 kg). The red-tailed hawk has a distinctive scream that is often heard in a variety of wild habitats.

The red-tailed hawk, native to North America, is the most common hawk on the continent. It was first used in falconry by American falconers during the twentieth century. This newcomer to the sport has proved itself an excellent falconry bird that is now popular worldwide.

In the wild, the red-tailed hawk eats small mammals of all kinds, from rabbits to mice. Hunting hawks can be trained to chase birds as

A red-tailed hawk soars above an open field. An adaptable bird, the red-tailed hawk occupies various habitats from the state of Alaska southward to Central America.

well. Red-tailed hawks often hunt by soaring for hours on end. They also perch high up on tree branches or even telephone poles, on the lookout for prey. Although they are powerful birds, red-tailed hawks are not as agile in the air as falcons.

American Kestrel

The American kestrel, or sparrow hawk, is the other bird generally flown by apprentices. Weighing just 3.5 ounces (0.1 kg), it is the smallest falcon in the United States. It is about the size of a robin. The American bird is not closely related to any European kestrels or sparrow hawks.

Wild kestrels eat mostly mice and insects, but they can be used to hunt small birds such as sparrows and starlings. Kestrels typically hunt by hovering over possible quarry and dropping down.

Some falconers are reluctant to recommend kestrels as an apprentice's first bird because they can be fragile and high-maintenance. Kestrels have a very fast metabolism. Some experts recommend weighing them three times each day and feeding them twice daily. Kestrels are also easily harmed by cats, dogs, the elements, and even rough handling.

Other Raptors

A variety of other raptors native to the United States are also employed in falconry. The ferruginous hawk is a buteo slightly larger than the red-tailed hawk. An accipiter called the goshawk is a popular hunting bird that pursues rabbits, squirrels, ducks,

Rufus, a Harris' hawk, makes regular rounds during the Wimbledon tennis tournament in England to scare away pigeons that might otherwise disrupt matches.

and geese—its name is derived from "goose hawk." Other accipiters used for hunting include the small sharp-shinned hawk and the slightly larger Cooper's hawk.

The gyrfalcon, one of the traditional hunting birds of European falconry and the largest falcon, is also found wild in the United States. It's used to hunt grouse, ducks, and other large birds. The prairie falcon is similar in size and appearance to the peregrine and hunts the same quarry, though falconers consider the two types of birds to have completely different temperaments. The merlin, a small true falcon, is best known for hunting pigeons.

The medium-sized Harris' hawk is the only member of the parabuteo classification of raptors. Native to the United States, it's unique in that it hunts cooperatively, generally in small family groups. Because

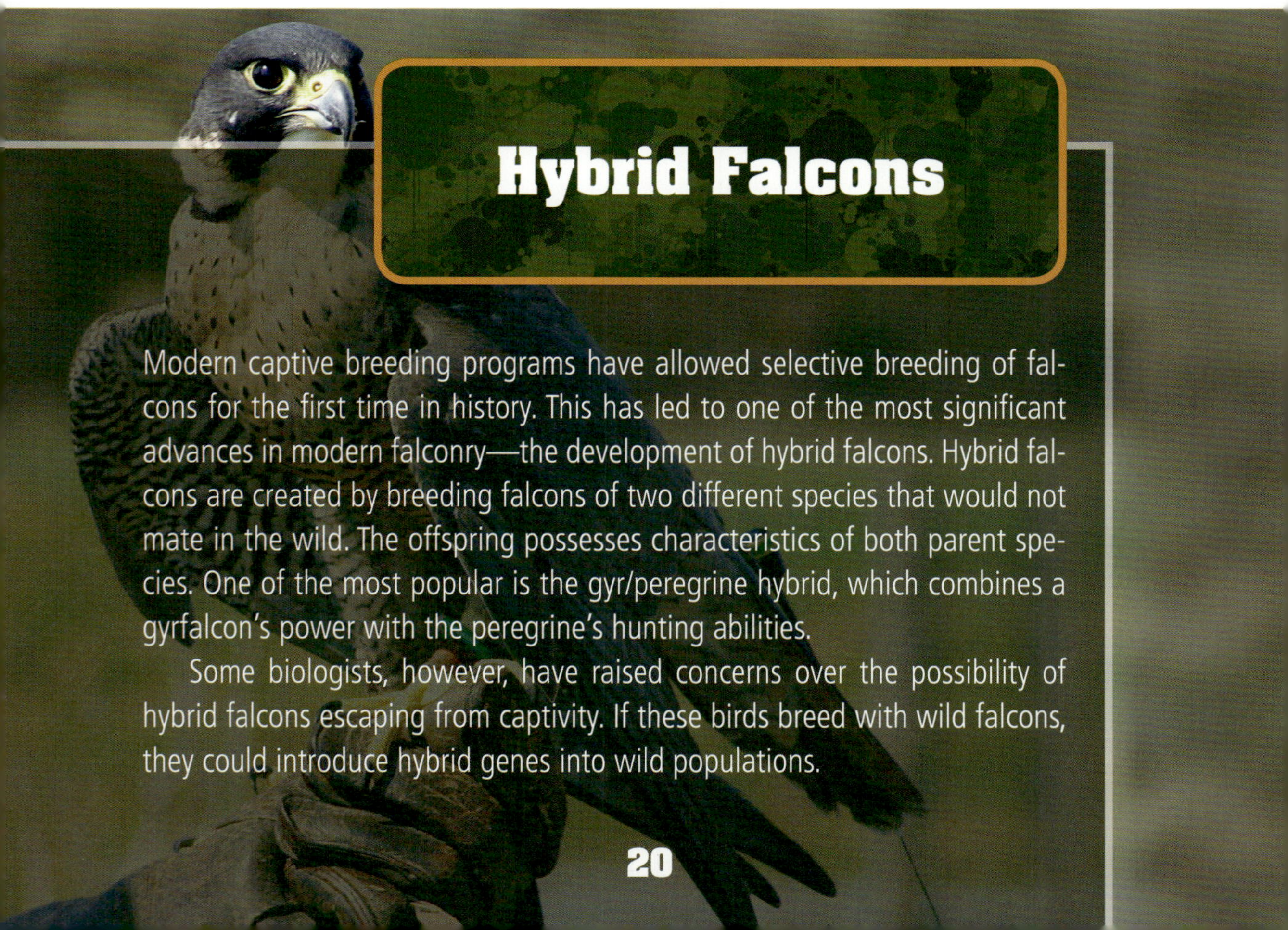

Hybrid Falcons

Modern captive breeding programs have allowed selective breeding of falcons for the first time in history. This has led to one of the most significant advances in modern falconry—the development of hybrid falcons. Hybrid falcons are created by breeding falcons of two different species that would not mate in the wild. The offspring possesses characteristics of both parent species. One of the most popular is the gyr/peregrine hybrid, which combines a gyrfalcon's power with the peregrine's hunting abilities.

Some biologists, however, have raised concerns over the possibility of hybrid falcons escaping from captivity. If these birds breed with wild falcons, they could introduce hybrid genes into wild populations.

of its social nature, the Harris' hawk adapts relatively easily to working with a falconer. It's a versatile and highly effective hunter that will chase quarry from rabbits to quail. Since being introduced by U.S. falconers, Harris' hawks have become highly popular hunting hawks internationally.

Bringing Home Your Falcon

An apprentice falconer generally traps his or her first raptor in the wild. The bird must be a passager, or passage bird—a young bird that is beginning her first autumn migration. Passagers can be identified by their easily recognized immature plumage.

There are several types of traps, which generally either snare the bird's foot in a noose or catch her in a net. Most traps require live bait, such as a pigeon or rodent that is restrained in a harness. The lure animal is often unharmed during the trapping, although there is the possibility that it will be hurt or killed. Falconers often rotate different bait animals during the trapping process to avoid causing unnecessary stress. The trap should be set in an area frequented by the birds. Falconers sometimes set up traps for red-tailed hawks near roads, although this can be dangerous.

Once trapped, falcons often go limp with shock. Other times, though, they fight the falconer when he or she comes near. The bird's talons and beak can cause significant injury. One trick used in removing the bird is to give her a rag to "foot," or claw at, as a distraction while reaching for the legs. The falconer may then hood the bird, though some handlers choose against hooding. Before taking the falcon home, it is important to check the bird's health.

Experienced falconers have a greater range of options in obtaining birds. In some states, general and master falconers can trap wild birds at stages other than passager. A haggard is a falcon captured as an

A licensed falconer in Montana holds an eyas ferruginous hawk that he took from a nest in early summer and plans to train for the fall hunting season.

adult. An eyas is a young bird taken from the nest. In addition, many falconers buy captive-bred falcons or breed their own. There are about four hundred licensed breeders in the United States. Any falconer should confirm that the breeder is reputable before committing to buy a bird by checking with falconry organizations and experienced falconers. (Moreover, a potential buyer should make sure that the breeder's license and relevant paperwork are current and visit the facilities if possible, although falcons are often shipped long distances.)

Falconers sometimes opt to hack an eyas, whether captive bred or wild caught. "Hacking" means releasing a bird into the wild. For training purposes, falconers may temporarily set the fledgling falcon free for up to a month or so before retrapping her. During this period of growth, the bird builds up strength and learns how to navigate the outdoors independently, which makes her a more effective hunting bird. The circumstances of the bird's freedom are as tightly supervised as possible. The young birds do not initially stray far and voluntarily return to the "hack box." The falconer provides food during the hacking process. Once the birds have learned to fly and hunt, they're retrapped using the same method as wild trapping. Despite precautions, there is the danger that the falconer will fail in retrapping and lose the bird.

CHAPTER 3

Care and Training

Falconry requires a substantial commitment of time and resources. An apprentice falconer may find the list of requirements and expenses daunting. A falcon is not a pet, and she cannot be kept in a cage and left to herself. Raptors are fierce and independent, yet captive falcons depend on their handlers to tend to their basic needs.

Before an apprentice acquires a bird, he or she must construct housing and acquire a considerable amount of specialized gear. Once the falcon arrives, it is a time of transition for both the bird and the falconer. Taming and training the hawk require long hours, patience, and discipline. For dedicated falconers, however, fostering a cooperative relationship with the bird is well worth the effort.

Facilities and Equipment

Falcons are housed in a building called a mews. A falconer should put great care into constructing and securing the falcon's mews. It must offer protection from the elements and any possible threats. Owls, dogs, cats, and even rats can kill or maim falcons.

A mews housing a single bird is generally at least 8 by 8 feet (2.4 by 2.4 meters) in area. It has at least one window fitted with vertical bars. A well-lit mews with multiple windows is not necessarily desirable, since falcons often prefer to be able to retreat to a dark corner. Also, the windows should be placed so that the interior will neither overheat nor leave the bird overexposed to cold winds. The floor must be well drained and allow easy cleaning. Several perches of different sizes should be installed at various heights and positions. A bath pan full of water, large enough to hold the hawk's body, should be available at all times. Some falcons enjoy playing with toys if they are provided.

The falcon may be tethered to a perch or allowed to fly free—"free lofted"—in the mews. Birds should not be free lofted until they have been trained to respond to the handler's signals.

In addition to the mews, a falconer must prepare an open-air facility called a weathering yard where the bird can spend time outdoors in fair weather. The weathering yard is constructed of sturdy fencing with the top covered by fencing, mesh, or roofing.

The equipment used by a falconer is sometimes referred to as "furniture." Many falconers prefer to make some of their gear by hand, which ensures good quality and a proper fit on the bird. Falconry equipment and accessories are also available commercially.

Falconers use straps called jesses to tether the bird and restrain her when being handled. A single jess is attached to each of the falcon's legs. Aylmeri jesses, the most commonly used type, consist of two pieces:

Jesses must be sized for a falcon's reach as well as factors such as tail length, perching arrangement, and behavior—some birds tear at the jesses.

anklets that are fitted with separate jess straps. There are many styles of jesses appropriate to different circumstances. Short, stiff jesses used outdoors will not get tangled in branches. Longer jesses will give the bird a greater reach when tethered to a perch. Many falconers craft jesses out of kangaroo leather, although synthetic materials are also appropriate.

A falcon is often put on a leash during handling or tethering. The ends of the jesses are attached to a piece of hardware called a swivel, which is attached to the leash. The swivel rotates freely, preventing the leash from becoming tangled. Falconers use a longer restraint line called a creance during training. This allows the falcon to make longer flights without the risk of losing the bird.

Traditionally, falconers attached bells to the falcon's feet during hunting to track her movements. Today, telemetry equipment allows falconers to locate falcons that have flown out of sight. A small battery-operated transmitter is attached to the bird's leg, tail, neck, or back. The falconer carries a receiver with an antenna that picks up the signal emitted by the transmitter.

A falconer sometimes places a hood, which covers the eyes, on the bird's head. The practice may sound cruel, but hooding the falcon actually calms her by blocking out visual stimuli. The hood encloses the entire head, with an opening for the beak. Straps on the back of the hood, called braces, are tightened to close the hood. Many hoods are hand crafted and elaborately decorated, but the most important factor is a good fit. If the hood fits badly, it can bruise or chafe the bird's skin.

A thick glove called a gauntlet is essential to protect the falconer's arm from the bird's talons. The falconer generally carries the bird on his or her nondominant hand. Some falconers purchase elaborate customized leather gauntlets, but an inexpensive welding glove can offer adequate protection.

Every falconer should own a reliable scale and weigh the bird regularly. Tracking a falcon's weight allows the falconer to monitor

A falcon models a $55,000 diamond-studded hood crafted by Italian falconer and equipment artisan Giancarlo Pirrotta and customized by a jewelry studio.

the bird's health and determine her ideal flying weight. It is a good idea to record the bird's weight in a daily logbook, along with other information such as diet, behavioral observations, and low weather temperatures for the day.

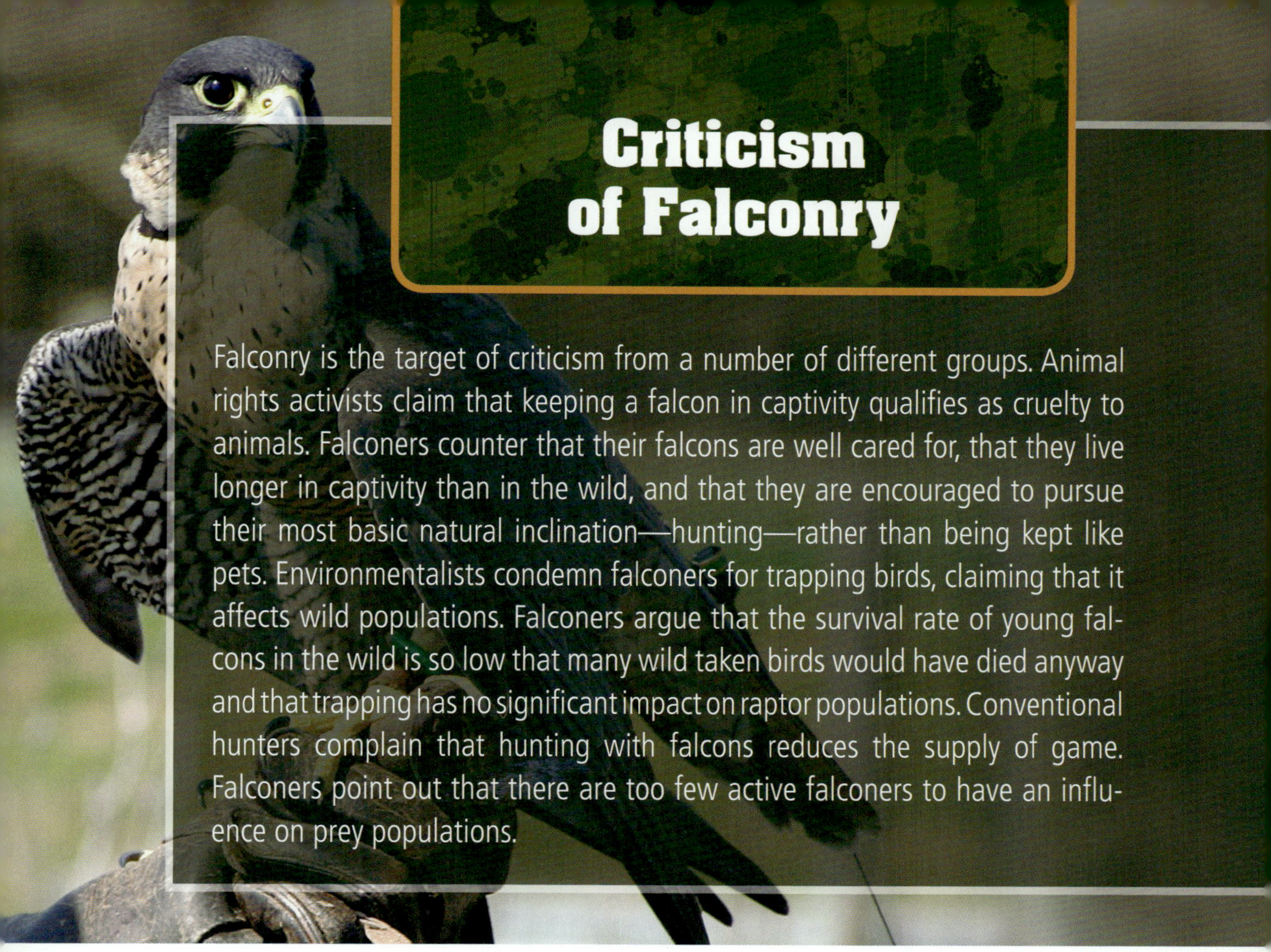

Criticism of Falconry

Falconry is the target of criticism from a number of different groups. Animal rights activists claim that keeping a falcon in captivity qualifies as cruelty to animals. Falconers counter that their falcons are well cared for, that they live longer in captivity than in the wild, and that they are encouraged to pursue their most basic natural inclination—hunting—rather than being kept like pets. Environmentalists condemn falconers for trapping birds, claiming that it affects wild populations. Falconers argue that the survival rate of young falcons in the wild is so low that many wild taken birds would have died anyway and that trapping has no significant impact on raptor populations. Conventional hunters complain that hunting with falcons reduces the supply of game. Falconers point out that there are too few active falconers to have an influence on prey populations.

Feeding and Health

A captive falcon should be fed a high-quality diet similar to what she would eat in the wild. Raw meat from a grocery store alone does not fulfill the nutritional requirements of raptors. The falconer should also vary the bird's diet—some possible foods include chicken necks, sparrows, game birds (such as duck, quail, or pigeon), mice, rabbits, squirrels, and chicks. Many falconers use pieces of beef heart for tidbits during handling. Smaller birds such as kestrels also eat insects. The falcon should be given whole game, since feathers, fur, and bones provide minerals and roughage that aids in digestion. A falcon's food can be kept frozen; it can be defrosted before feeding.

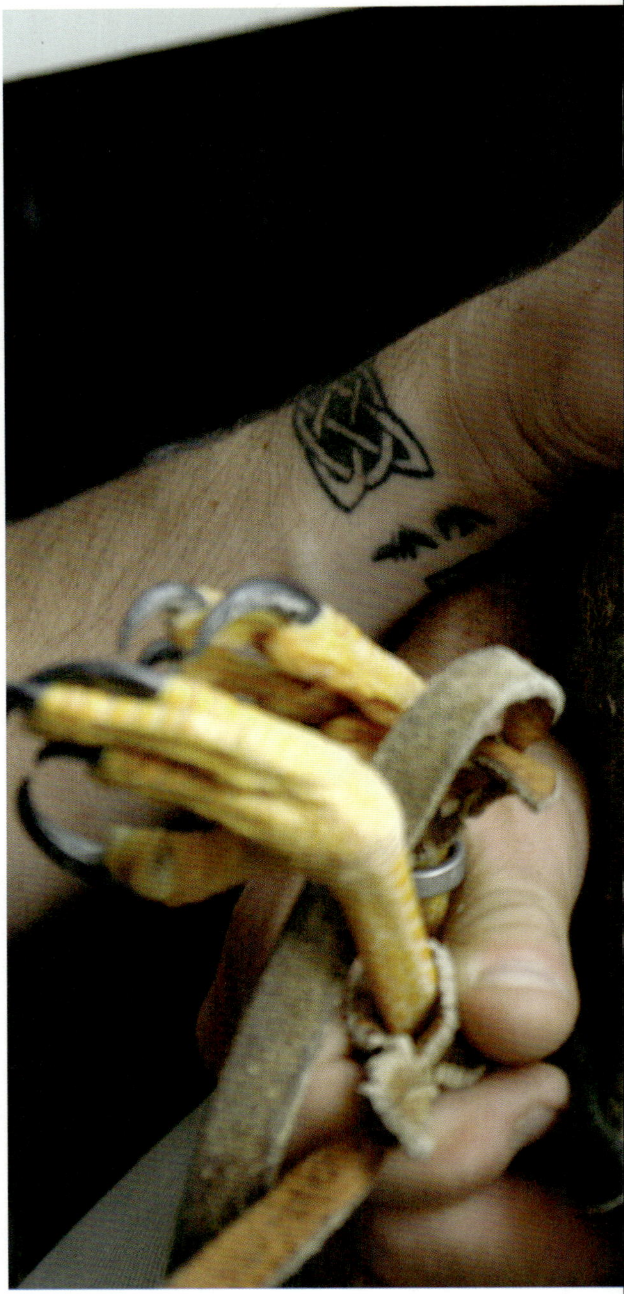

The falconer should consider the diet of the game being given to the falcon and buy from a reliable source. Game available commercially is sometimes given low-quality feed and is dosed with supplements. Some serious falconers raise their own game as food for their birds.

Just as falconers carefully track the weight of their falcons, they also weigh the falcon's food. A bird requires a certain number of calories daily to maintain an ideal weight. Experienced falconers can gauge a falcon's physical condition by feeling the bird's breastbone. Falconers generally feed their falcons every day, although not all raptors eat daily in the wild. The falconer will adjust the amount of food depending on factors such as the bird's level of activity or outdoor temperature. The day before a hunt, the falconer will cut the normal allotment of food.

Falcons require a great deal of maintenance, some of which may come as a surprise to apprentices. Captive birds may have to have their beak periodically reshaped—a process called coping—because they do not wear down their beak tearing

Visitors to the medieval town of Provins, France, can attend an aerial falconry show and visit the aviary. Here, a Provins falconer copes a bird's beak with a file.

tough food as occurs in the wild. Falconers also trim and shape the bird's talons. Only experienced falconers should work on the falcon's beak and talons. The mews must be regularly cleaned, and the falconer should take notice of abnormal mutes—fecal matter—that might indicate disease or illness. The bird also spits up castings, which are the indigestible parts of its food, such as fur and bones. A falconer may exercise the falcon, such as by having her fly up to the glove repeatedly, to keep her in good condition.

A falconer must monitor the bird's health closely for any signs of sickness, which may be indicated by physical symptoms or behavioral changes. The falconer should be familiar with the signs of typical ailments, such as parasites, poor nutrition, viruses, and infections, and watch for any scratches or lesions near the beak or feet that could become infected. The falconer should also pay attention to any equipment or housing issues that could affect the bird's health. If a perch irritates the feet, for example, it should be replaced. If the mews overheats during the day, blinds in front of a window might be necessary. In particular, the falconer should take care to prevent damage to the bird's feathers.

The falconer may be able to treat minor ailments at home. A case of feather lice, for example, can be dealt with by an insecticide spray. In case of serious illnesses and health emergencies, the bird should be taken to the veterinarian immediately. Avian veterinary medicine is a specialty, so not all vets are qualified to treat raptors. The falconer should locate the nearest experienced avian veterinarian before a crisis makes veterinary care necessary.

Training the Falcon

A newly acquired falcon will be wary of human beings. The first step in training a falcon is demonstrating that humans pose no threat and provide food. A falcon's appetite is a significant motivator in training and hunting. This does not mean that the falconer starves the bird. At her peak flying weight, the falcon is hungry, eager, and physically responsive. A heavy bird that has recently gorged itself on food will not be in good shape for hunting. During training, the falconer does not teach the bird new behaviors so much as shape her natural tendencies as a predator. The bird learns that she and the falconer share interests that provide for her needs. Punishment is not effective in falconry because it's not in a falcon's nature to behave submissively toward a dominant figure.

The traditional method for taming a new falcon is "manning" the bird. The falcon is immersed in her new human environment while she is still in a state of shock at being captured. The falconer carries her around for hours and even days on end until she is tired out, introducing her to new sights and experiences. A new, nervous falcon may frequently "bate," which is the falconry term for when the bird attempts to fly away and is caught short by the leash. Through the manning process, the falcon becomes accustomed to people, dogs, cars, and other aspects of daily life.

As soon as possible, the falconer begins feeding the new bird. Early on, the falcon is unwilling to bend down her head to eat in a human's presence. In the wild, this position renders her vulnerable to attack. Eating in the falconer's presence indicates trust. The falconer can induce her to eat by tempting her with small tidbits of diced meat and popping them in her beak when she opens her mouth.

Once the falcon is tamed and receptive to food, she must be taught to respond to signals. It is very important that the falconer be consistent during training. If the trainer is inconsistent with cues and rewards, the falcon will not respond consistently. The falcon is gradually coaxed with food to approach the trainer on a perch. The next step is to teach the bird to jump to the falconer's gloved hand on command, which is accomplished by tempting her with food. Falconers often teach their birds to associate a whistle with food. As a result, the falcon associates a whistle with the reward and responds to the cue. Eventually, the falcon learns to recognize other cues as well. She will respond to the falconer's voice and jump to the glove when the falconer extends his or her glove. Once the falcon begins flying longer distances to the fist, she is ready for outdoor training on the creance.

A piece of fake prey called a lure is a valuable tool in training and on the field. The lure is made of feathers or fur to mimic the falcon's intended quarry, and often a piece of meat is tied to it. The falconer attaches the lure to a long line during training. The falcon learns to associate the lure with a substantial reward of food. She will fly to the lure when it is laid on the ground and, later, when it is twirled in the air or trailed on the ground. Often the falconer uses a special whistle distinct from the usual cue when bringing out the lure. The falcon learns that the lure is the ultimate reward, and the falconer employs the lure during the hunt as a sure means of retrieving the bird. Handlers teach true falcons—though generally not other raptors such as hawks—to stoop to the lure, or plunge down, during training.

Once the falcon is responsive to the lure, the falconer removes the creance and allows her to fly free. The training continues as before,

A peregrine falcon chases a lure thrown by the falconer. A lure should be made of lightweight material with no holes or exposed metal parts that could injure the bird.

except that the bird now has a greater range of flight. Sometimes falconers prepare the falcon for the hunt by introducing dead or live game. The falcon may "hunt" a dead rabbit being pulled at the end of a creance, for example, or she may be allowed to kill domestic rabbits or birds released for her to chase.

Slightly different training methods are used for different species of raptors. Hawks, for example, are generally more willing to return to the glove than falcons, which respond better to the lure. In addition, each bird has its own personality. Experienced falconers learn to recognize personality traits and employ training techniques that will be effective for the individual bird.

It takes about a month to prepare a falcon for hunting in the field. Training continues even after the hunt has begun because learning to work together effectively is an ongoing process for the falconer and falcon.

CHAPTER 4

ON THE HUNT

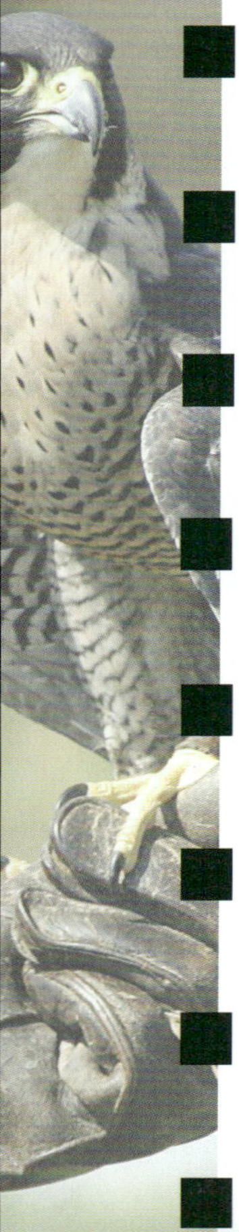

Once the falcon has been trained, she is ready to be taken into the field. A bird's first hunt is a momentous event for apprentice and experienced falconers alike.

Falconry is not a sport for half-hearted hunters. The falconer must prove his or her dedication to the goal of catching game. The falconer's job is to locate game for the bird to pursue. This requires considerable knowledge of the quarry, its behavior, and the habitat. Many serious falconers hunt with dogs, such as pointers, which locate and flush the quarry on command. Training and handling hunting dogs are considerable undertakings. The falconer should also consider the terrain and choose areas that favor the bird's chances of successfully bringing down prey.

During hunting season, a falcon should be taken hunting at least twice every week.

Falconry clubs generally recommend taking the bird out three to six times a week. Dedicated falconers hunt daily and may also travel to attend hunting meets or hunt on exceptional hunting grounds.

Getting Ready

The hunt can be an all-day activity, although it is more likely to last two to four hours. Preparations begin the previous day. The falcon receives only a partial ration of food. The falconer checks that the gear is in good condition and plans the hunt. Preparations tend to become routine once the season is underway, but the falconer should learn from experiences and observations in the field and adjust hunting practices accordingly.

Many falconers rise very early in the morning to be in the field at dawn, although this is not imperative. Teenage apprentices can successfully take the bird out hunting after school. Nonetheless, the hunt should be called off when dusk approaches. If the bird were to become lost, it would be much more difficult to search in the dark.

The falconer should pack a bag or hunting vest with equipment like spare leashes and jesses and copies of paperwork, such as licenses and permits. He or she should also bring a bag of meat tidbits for motivating the bird,

Florida biologist and falconer Adam Grayson, who is wearing a hawking bag, hunts in the field with his Aplomado falcon. He compares caring for a falcon to managing a prizefighter.

the lure, the glove, and a telemetry receiver, as well as a water bottle, snacks, hunting knife, and first-aid kit.

A falcon is transported in a carrier called a hawk box or a giant hood. The bird should be introduced to the hawk box and driven around in the car ahead of the first hunt. The falconer may hood the bird while transporting her to the field, depending on the bird's personality and the falconer's handling philosophy.

For the hunt, the falcon is equipped with short field jesses, bells, and a telemetry transmitter. The falconer should check the batteries in the transmitter and confirm that it is receiving a signal properly before "casting off" the bird, or sending it airborne by lifting the wrist.

In the Field

A falcon's hunting behavior in the field depends on a variety of factors, including the weather and terrain, the species of raptor, and the bird's personality. A falcon sometimes enters a mentally and physically focused state called "yarak" while on the hunt. Once in the air, the bird takes position to watch for prey. She may circle around high in the air or take up a position in a nearby tall tree. True falcons are attack birds, and they don't range on their own in search of prey. As the falconer moves around on the ground, the falcon follows along. Early on, the falconer may have to encourage the bird by calling her down and letting her up into the air again until she learns to keep pace.

On some hunts, the falconer waits until there is sure quarry nearby before casting off the bird. Once the falcon has reached a good position, the falconer flushes the quarry for the bird to attack. If the bird misses, the falconer calls the bird back and moves to another field to give her a second chance. Another tactic is to cast off the bird before finding quarry and letting the hawk wait on—soar overhead—while the falconer scouts below. This technique requires significant stamina

A falcon stoops to the quarry. After the bird brings down its prey, such as a dove, the handler swaps it for tidbits of meat.

from the bird and it increases the risk of losing the bird while she is high aloft.

To make a catch, the peregrine falcon stoops to the quarry and almost always takes prey in midair. She hits the target with claws open in a dive that gives lethal momentum to the slashing blow. Because of these tactics, falcons can take down prey that is over three times their own weight. Hawks, by contrast, seize and kill prey with their long, powerful talons. Male and female birds also have different hunting styles. The smaller tiercel peregrine falcon, for example, moves faster and climbs higher in the air than the larger female.

Each bird has her own quirks in the field. Some birds are more aggressive than others. A falcon may prefer a particular type of quarry and refuse to chase anything else. Falconers tend to admire birds that ascend quickly and hit the prey with a single knockout blow. If the falcon descends slowly or fails to reach a lofty height, the prey is more likely to observe the bird and flee. If the falcon fails to nail the quarry with her strike, the prey is more likely to escape. Overall, a bird's performance in the field depends on individual aptitude and training.

A falconer uses a telemetry transmitter to search for a falcon lost during a hunt. The unit emits beeps that provide a means of tracking the falcon's movements.

The falcon does not make a catch on every hunt, and things can easily go wrong. Every falconer dreads the possibility of losing a bird. A falcon soaring up high on an air current can be swept out of sight. A bird chasing prey can fly out of range of the falconer's cues. In some cases, poor training may be to blame in losing a bird. Other times, a reliable falcon may fail to respond for no identifiable reason. When a bird becomes lost, the falconer tracks her using the telemetry receiver. The signals eventually lead the falconer to the bird. Occasionally, however, telemetry tracking fails. The bird may fly out of range of the receiver or lose the transmitter. (Many falconers attach two transmitters in case one fails or is lost.) The falconer may patrol the roads in a vehicle hoping to pick up a signal. In *Equinox*, the avid falconer Dan O'Brien describes renting an airplane to search for a telemetry signal from a lost bird. Nonetheless, falconers sometimes lose a bird for good despite every effort to recover her.

Even worse is the possibility of having a falcon injured or killed in the field. Golden eagles can kill falcons, especially when they are on the ground distracted by a catch. Falcons can be electrocuted on power lines or killed in freak accidents, such as being hit by a car. It's not unheard of for falcons to be shot, either in error or intentionally. Sometimes a falconer may be confronted by conventional hunters or local residents hostile to hawk hunting. In these types of tense situations, the best course of action is to avoid conflict and walk away, even when in accordance with the law.

After the Catch

A falcon that has made a catch does not return to the falconer with the prey. Instead, the falconer must go to the bird to retrieve the game. He or she takes the game from the bird and exchanges it for a smaller piece of meat. If the prey is still alive, the falconer dispatches it quickly and humanely.

A peregrine falcon tears at its meal. Falcons kill their prey in midair by severing the spinal cord with their sharp hooked beaks.

Depending on what the falcon has caught, the falconer may plan to have the game for dinner. Alternately, the falconer may put the catch in the freezer for the bird's future meals.

A falcon cannot be controlled after she has been cast off, and falcons sometimes bring down prey that is out of season. When this occurs, the falconer must leave the game in the field. If the bird kills prey that belongs to a threatened or endangered species, it must be reported to government wildlife authorities.

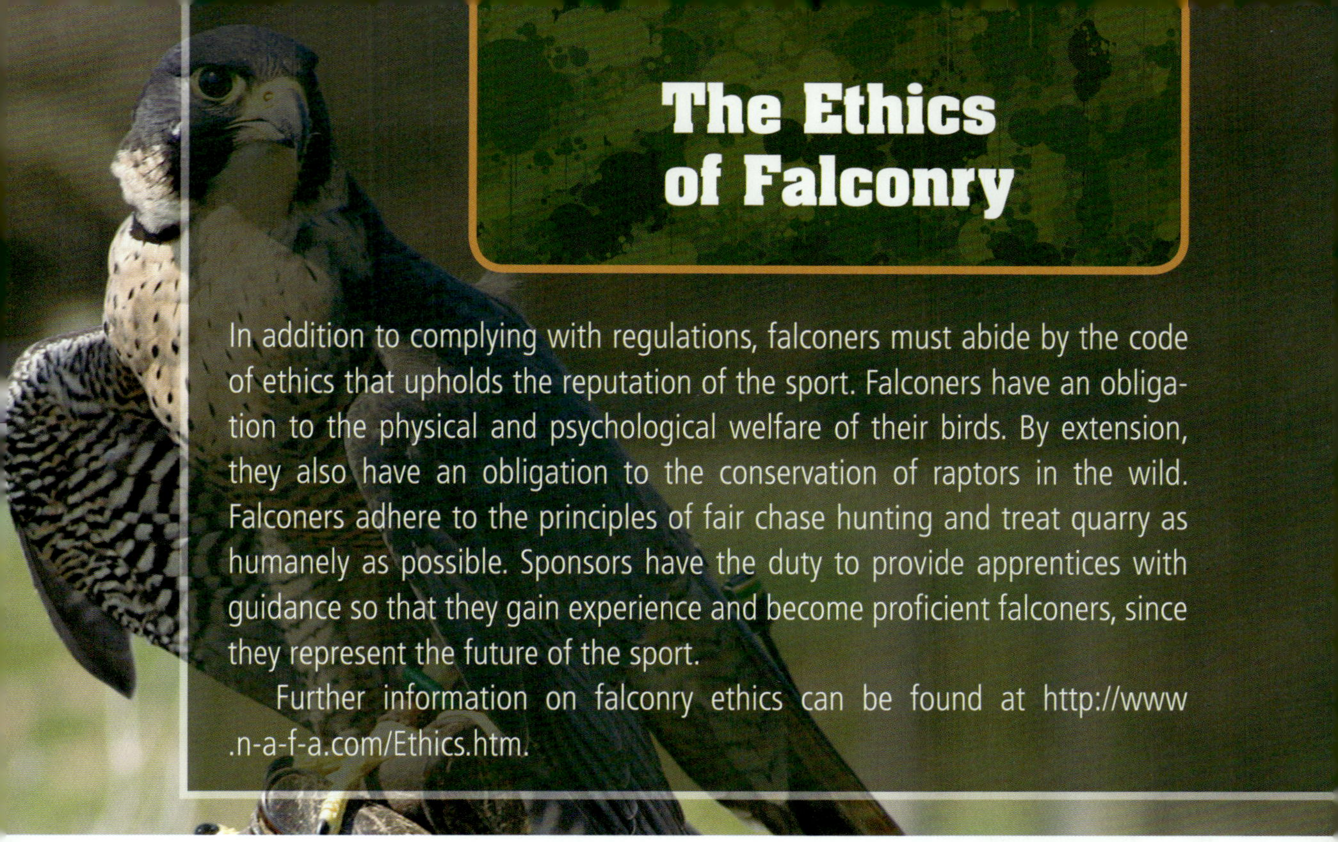

The Ethics of Falconry

In addition to complying with regulations, falconers must abide by the code of ethics that upholds the reputation of the sport. Falconers have an obligation to the physical and psychological welfare of their birds. By extension, they also have an obligation to the conservation of raptors in the wild. Falconers adhere to the principles of fair chase hunting and treat quarry as humanely as possible. Sponsors have the duty to provide apprentices with guidance so that they gain experience and become proficient falconers, since they represent the future of the sport.

Further information on falconry ethics can be found at http://www.n-a-f-a.com/Ethics.htm.

Off-Season

Specific dates for falconry game seasons vary from one state to another. In general, they extend for several months through the autumn and winter. Many falconers cut back on hunting during regular firearm season.

After the hunting season is over, the bird molts, or sheds and regrows her feathers. The bird can easily be stressed during molting, so the falconer generally leaves her in the mews—or "intermews" her—with minimal handling during the process. Birds tend to act aloof and uncooperative during this period and have to be reminded of their training for the next hunting season.

A falconer sometimes chooses to hack a bird permanently back into the wild after the end of the hunting season. The best time to release a raptor is spring or early summer, when there is ample game. A falcon should be released in a wilderness area far from any human activity.

CHAPTER 5

REGULATIONS AND RESPONSIBILITIES

Before becoming actively involved in falconry, an aspiring apprentice falconer should read and take careful note of the regulations governing the sport. Otherwise, it could be possible to inadvertently violate the law. Falconry regulations cover a wide variety of areas, from acquiring equipment and housing to trapping the bird and seeing to its daily care. Some rules are highly esoteric. For example, it is illegal to possess hawk feathers for any purpose other than "imping," or repairing feathers of captive birds.

Falconry is legal in every state except for Hawaii and Washington, D.C. Many falconers fly their birds on public land, either federal or state-owned. Some public land may be restricted for hunting, however, so a falconer should confirm that falconry is legal at a particular site before setting out on the hunt. In addition,

Alan Pope, president of the Indiana Falconers Association, holds his northern goshawk while describing some of the regulations that falconers must follow—not only to own a bird of prey but also to hunt with one.

falconers should always get permission before stepping onto privately owned land. When hunting on private land, falconers should carry a note from the landowner formally granting permission in case of questioning by the authorities.

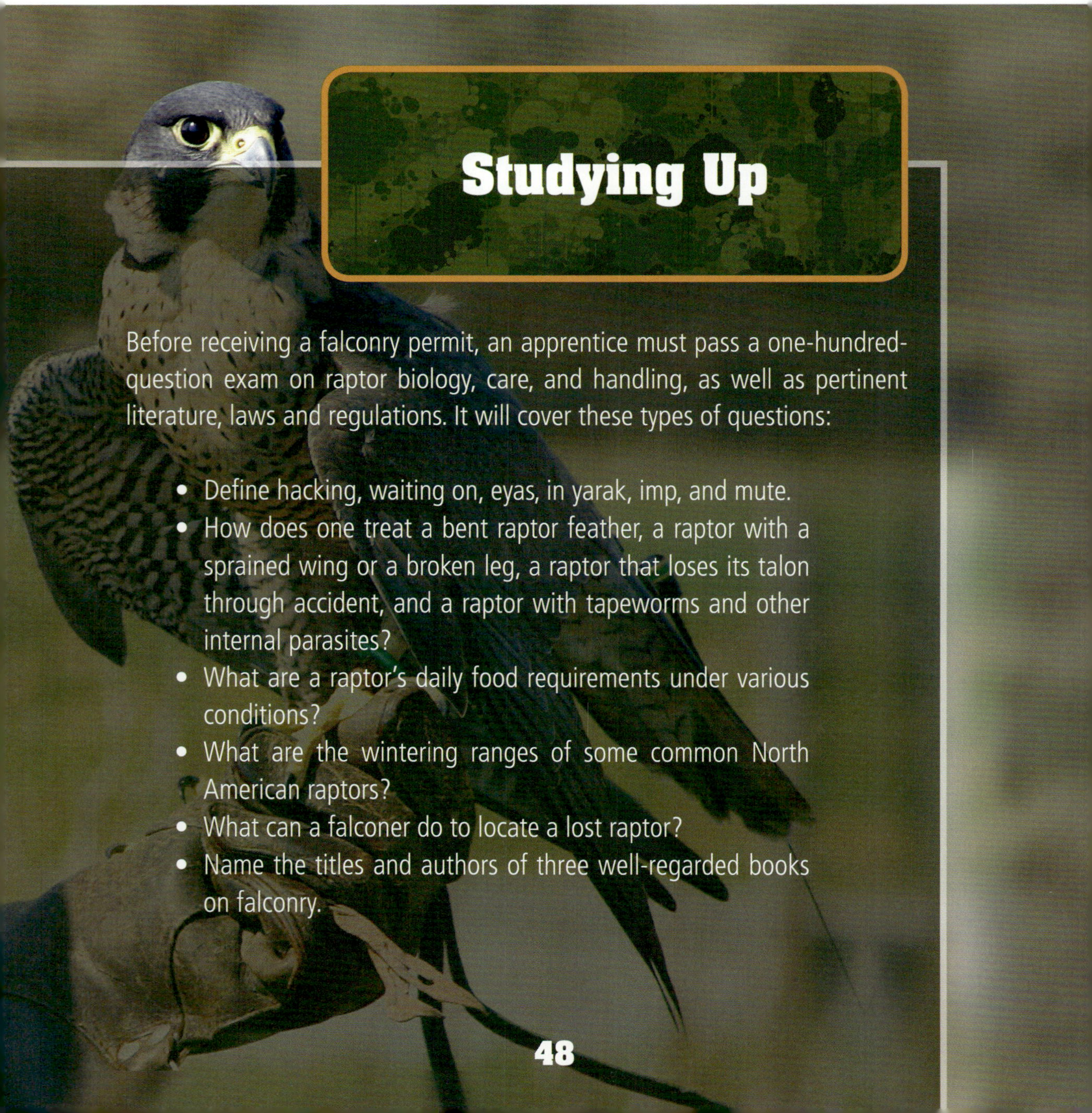

Studying Up

Before receiving a falconry permit, an apprentice must pass a one-hundred-question exam on raptor biology, care, and handling, as well as pertinent literature, laws and regulations. It will cover these types of questions:

- Define hacking, waiting on, eyas, in yarak, imp, and mute.
- How does one treat a bent raptor feather, a raptor with a sprained wing or a broken leg, a raptor that loses its talon through accident, and a raptor with tapeworms and other internal parasites?
- What are a raptor's daily food requirements under various conditions?
- What are the wintering ranges of some common North American raptors?
- What can a falconer do to locate a lost raptor?
- Name the titles and authors of three well-regarded books on falconry.

Know the Law

Falconry is regulated by the U.S. Fish and Wildlife Service under the Migratory Bird Treaty Act. In 2008, the federal falconry regulations were significantly revised. Under the new rules, the federal government ceased issuing falconry permits. Instead, individual states would issue permits in compliance with federal standards. The new regulations set a 2014 deadline for states to set up administration of falconry permitting programs.

The new federal rules relaxed many requirements for apprentices. In the past, apprentices had to trap their own bird in the wild, and they were only permitted to fly a red-tailed hawk or a kestrel. According to the new rules, apprentices may trap and fly a larger range of native raptors. An apprentice's first bird can now be either trapped in the wild or captive bred. The minimum age of apprenticeship was lowered from fourteen to twelve.

In addition to federal law, falconers must comply with state laws. In most states, falconry is overseen by the natural resources department. State laws concerning apprenticeships are sometimes more strict than the new federal standards. Many states provide an informational packet for prospective apprentices. State and regional falconry clubs may also offer relevant information on their Web sites for people interested in becoming falconers.

Federal and state laws address nearly every step in the process of completing an apprenticeship. First, the aspiring apprentice must pass a comprehensive one-hundred-question exam with a score of at least 80 percent. Before acquiring the falcon, the apprentice must acquire falconry gear and construct the mews and weathering yard. Falconers must hold a hunting license as well as a falconry permit—an apprentice must have a sponsor who will sign the falconry permit application. Trapping a falcon requires a trapping permit. Captive birds must wear an identifying band on their legs. In addition, it is a good idea for apprentices to join their regional falconry club, which can provide valuable resources.

Sponsorship and Apprenticeship

Under federal law, there are three classes of falconers: apprentice, general, and master. An apprentice must be sponsored by a general or master falconer, and an apprenticeship lasts at least two years. An apprentice is permitted to possess only one bird, and an apprentice is only allowed to trap passager birds.

An apprentice falconer becomes a general falconer after successfully completing the apprenticeship and submitting a document of approval from his or her sponsor. A general falconer must be at least sixteen years old. General falconers are permitted to possess three birds. After five years, a general falconer can qualify as a master falconer. Master falconers are permitted to possess five birds. General

Falconry demands a high degree of personal responsibility, but many experienced falconers describe falconry as a passion that took root at a young age.

and master falconers are allowed to trap eyasses as well as passagers, although federal and state laws restrict the number and type of birds that can be taken legally.

An apprentice's sponsor acts as a mentor as the apprentice learns how to care for, handle, and train a falcon. Many aspects of falconry cannot be learned from books, and an experienced falconer can guide the apprentice through unexpected difficulties. A sponsor can also help the apprentice navigate the regulations and ethics of falconry.

An aspiring apprentice can connect with prospective sponsors through a state or regional falconry club. Acting as a sponsor is a major commitment for a falconer, however—a falconer will only sponsor apprentices who he or she believes are committed and capable of mastering falconry. Some sponsors require a year of preapprentice time in the field and a formal contract of apprentices.

Paying the Price and Taking the Time

A prospective apprentice falconer will thoroughly prepare for acquiring a falcon. He or she will spend time hunting with an experienced falconer, master the material necessary for passing the state falconry exam, and apply for the necessary licenses and permits. Such preparation tends to eliminate dabblers who are squeamish about dealing with bad-tempered and aggressive birds, cleaning out the mews, handling raw meat to feed the raptors, or retrieving bloody torn-up game from the bird.

Still, aspiring apprentices should consider the long-term commitment required of falconers. Falconry is not an inexpensive undertaking. Before acquiring a bird, the falconer must construct a mews and acquire gear. At minimum, the initial costs will exceed $500, and they could reach $2,000 or more. An apprentice can cut costs by buying inexpensive equipment and building materials whenever possible, but good-quality products are often worth the investment. Cheap, badly fitting gear and a shoddy mews can have negative health consequences for the bird. Even after the bird has arrived, the apprentice will still have to pay for food and other ongoing costs. In addition, there are application and renewal fees for licenses, permits, and club memberships.

The apprentice must also make a time commitment to the falcon. Daily care requires less than an hour's time, but a falconer does not have the option of skipping it on a busy day. The falconer must be genuinely enthusiastic about taking the bird hunting at least several times every week as well. An apprentice can get away with occasionally skipping hunting due to a busy schedule or bad weather, but the bird will suffer if it becomes a regular occurrence. Falconry can be a highly rewarding experience, and many seasoned falconers became involved in the sport during high school, but the responsibilities involved should not be taken lightly.

GLOSSARY

accipiter A genus of raptors with short, broad wings and narrow tails.

buteo A genus of raptors with broad wings used for soaring.

carnivorous Feeding on other animals.

cast off To launch the bird into the air off the fist.

creance A long line attached to a raptor during early training flights.

dispatch To kill with quick efficiency.

eradicate To destroy completely.

eyas A nestling raptor.

fecal matter Waste matter that is discharged from the bowels after food is digested.

fledgling An immature bird learning how to fly.

flush To drive a game bird or animal from its cover.

gauntlet A heavy glove used to carry a falcon.

hack To release a falcon into the wild, either permanently or temporarily for training purposes.

haggard A wild adult raptor.

hood The cap used to cover a trained raptor's head and serve as a blindfold.

hybrid The offspring resulting from the cross between parents of different species or subspecies.

imp To mend a broken feather on a raptor by splicing on an undamaged feather.

intermew To keep a trained raptor in captivity during molting.

jesses The straps attached to a trained raptor's legs for handling.

lure A fake quarry attached to a line that is used to train and call back trained raptors.

manning The process of acclimating a bird to human contact.

metabolism The chemical processes that occur within a living organism to maintain life.

mews The living area where trained raptors are housed.
molt A bird's annual shedding and regrowing of feathers.
mute Hawk droppings.
passager A raptor in first-year plumage trapped during migration.
plumage A bird's feathers.
quarry The game pursued by a trained raptor.
stoop A falcon's fast, head-first dive from high above.
talon A raptor claw.
telemetry Radio tracking by means of a transmitter attached to the bird and a receiver operated by the handler.
tenacious Not readily letting go of, or giving up, an object, position, or principle.
tiercel A male raptor.

For More Information

California Hawking Club
Web site: http://www.calhawkingclub.org
This is the largest state club in the country devoted to falconry.

Canadian Parks and Wilderness Society
506–250 City Centre Avenue
Ottawa, ON K1R 6K7
Canada
(800) 333-9453
Web site: http://www.cpaws.org
The society focuses on protecting many important areas of Canada's wilderness.

Environment Canada
Inquiry Centre
10 Wellington, 23rd Floor
Gatineau, QC K1A 0H3
Canada
(819) 997-2800
Web site: http://www.ec.gc.ca
This is Canada's government agency that is charged with environmental protection and conservation.

International Association for Falconry and Conservation of Birds of Prey
Web site: http://www.i-a-f.org
This international organization is dedicated to preserving falconry and promoting conservation. It also promotes ecological studies and veterinary research involving birds of prey and domestic breeding of falcons.

North American Falconers Association
Web site: http://www.n-a-f-a.com
This association is the leading falconry organization in the country.

Peregrine Fund
5668 West Flying Hawk Lane
Boise, ID 83709
(208) 362-3716
Web site: http://www.peregrinefund.org
This organization was founded to save the peregrine falcon from extinction and now works to conserve birds of prey worldwide.

U.S. Fish and Wildlife Service
1849 C Street NW
Washington, DC 20240
(800) 344-9453
Web site: http://www.fws.gov
This federal agency is dedicated to the conservation, protection, and enhancement of wildlife and plants and their habitats in the United States.

Web Sites

Due to the changing nature of Internet links, Rosen Publishing has developed an online list of Web sites related to the subject of this book. This site is updated regularly. Please use this link to access the list:

http://www.rosenlinks.com/HUNT/Falco

For Further Reading

Arent, Lori. *Raptors in Captivity: Guidelines for Care and Management*. Blaine, WA: Hancock House Publishing, 2007.

Bodio, Stephen J. *Eagle Dreams: Searching for Legends in Wild Mongolia*. Wiltshire, England: Crowood Press, 2006.

Capainolo, Peter, and Carol A. Butler. *How Fast Can a Falcon Dive? Fascinating Answers to Questions About Birds of Prey*. New Brunswick, NJ: Rutgers University Press, 2010.

Craighead, Frank, and John Craighead. *Hawks in the Hand: Adventures in Photography and Falconry*. New York, NY: Lyons Press, 1997.

Davis, Kate. *Falcons of North America*. Missoula, MT: Mountain Press Publishing, 2008.

Dunne, Pete. *Peter Dunne's Essential Field Guide Companion*. Boston, MA: Houghton Mifflin, 2006.

Dunne, Pete. *The Wind Masters: The Lives of North American Birds of Prey*. Boston, MA: Houghton Mifflin, 2003.

Dunne, Pete, David Sibley, and Clay Sutton. *Hawks in Flight: The Flight Identification of North American Migrant Raptors*. Boston, MA: Houghton Mifflin, 1988.

Fox, Nic. *Understanding the Bird of Prey.* Blaine, WA: Hancock House, 1995.

George, Jean Craighead. *My Side of the Mountain*. New York, NY: Puffin Books, 2004.

Glasier, Philip. *Falconry and Hawking*. 3rd ed. London, England: Batsford, 2006.

Haak, Bruce A. *The Hunting Falcon*. Blaine, WA: Hancock House, 1992.

Hallgarth, Adrian. *Hawking and Falconry for Beginners*. Blaine, WA: Hancock House, 2004.

Holderman, F. W. (ed.). *Apprentice Study Guide*. Fresno, CA: California Hawking Club, 1998.

McKay, James. *Practical Falconry*. London, England: Quiller Press, 2009.

O'Brien, Dan. *The Rites of Autumn: A Falconer's Journey Across the American West*. New York, NY: Lyons & Burford, 1997.

Parry-Jones, Jemima. *Eagle and Birds of Prey*. New York, NY: DK, 1997.

Savage, Candace. *Peregrine Falcons*. San Francisco, CA: Sierra Club Books for Children, 1993.

Snyder, Noel, and Helen Snyder. *Raptors of North America*. St. Paul, MN: Voyageur Press, 2006.

Straka, Andy. *A Witness Above*. Paradise, CA: Cedar Creek Publishing, 2011.

Walker, Adrian. *The Encyclopedia of Falconry*. New York, NY: Derrydale Press, 2000.

Wheeler, Brian K., and William S. Clark. *A Photographic Guide to North American Raptors*. San Diego, CA: Academic Press, 1996.

White, T. H. *The Once and Future King*. New York, NY: Ace Books, 1996.

Wright, Steve. *Falconry: The Essential Guide*. Ramsbury, England: Crowood Press, 2006.

Bibliography

ap Evans, Humphrey. *Falconry: An Illustrated Introduction*. New York, NY: Arco Publishing, 1973.

Bebee, Frank Lyman, and Harold Melvin Webster. *North American Falconry and Hunting Hawks*. Denver, CO: North American Falconry and Hunting Hawks, 1994.

"The Birds of North America Online." Ithaca, NY: Cornell Lab of Ornithology. Retrieved April 3, 2012 (http://bna.birds.Cornell.edu/bna).

Cocking, Susan. "Falconers Keep Sport of Kings Alive." *Standard-Examiner*, November 4, 2010. Retrieved April 4, 2012 (http://www.standard.net/topics/sports/2010/11/04/falconers-keep-sport-kings-alive).

"Code of Federal Regulations, Title 50: Wildlife and Fisheries Part 21—Migratory Bird Permits." Retrieved April 3, 2012 (http://ecfr.gpoaccess.gov/cgi/t/text/text-idx?c=ecfr&tpl=/ecfrbrowse/Title50/50cfr21_main_02.tpl).

Dickinson, Rachel. *Falconer on the Edge*. Boston, MA: Houghton Mifflin Harcourt, 2009.

Gallagher, Tim. *Falcon Fever: A Falconer in the Twenty-first Century*. Boston, MA: Houghton Mifflin, 2008.

Grossman, Mary Louise, and John Hamlet. *Birds of Prey of the World*. New York, NY: Random House, 1988.

Johnsgard, Paul A. *Hawks, Eagles, and Falcons of North America*. Washington, DC: Smithsonian Institution Press, 1990.

Mavrogordato, Jack. *A Hawk for the Bush*. New York, NY: Clarkson Potter, 1973.

"The Modern Apprentice: Falconry, Ecology, Education." Retrieved April 3, 2012 (http://www.themodernapprentice.com).

Oakes, William C. *The Falconer's Apprentice*. Warrens, WI: EagleWing Publishing, 2002.

O'Brien, Dan. *Equinox: Life, Love, and Birds of Prey*. New York, NY: Lyons & Burford, 1997.

Oggins, Robin S. *The Kings and Their Hawks: Falconry in Medieval England*. New Haven, CT: Yale University Press, 2004.

Tennesen, Michael. *Flight of the Falcon*. Toronto, ON, Canada: Key Porter Books, 1992.

Tutton, Mark. "Inside Abu Dhabi's State-of-the-Art Falcon Hospital." CNN.com, June 10, 2010. Retrieved April 2, 2012 (http://articles.cnn.com/2010-06-10/world/falcon.hospital.uae_1_falconry-uae-emirati?_s=PM:WORLD).

Weidensaul, Scott. *The Raptor Almanac: A Comprehensive Guide to Eagles, Hawks, Falcons, and Vultures*. New York, NY: Lyons Press, 2000.

Wingmasters. "A Description and History of Falconry." Retrieved April 3, 2012 (http://www.wingmasters.net/falconry_history.htm).

Index